# DOLPHINS!

## CARI JACKSON

# DOLPHINS!

Published by Liberty Street,
an imprint of Time Inc. Books,
a division of Meredith Corporation
225 Liberty Street
New York, NY 10281

**LIBERTY**
S T R E E T

LIBERTY STREET is a trademark of Time Inc.

ISBN: 978-1-68330-853-9

First edition, 2018
1 QGV 18
10 9 8 7 6 5 4 3 2 1

Produced by Scout Books & Media Inc

We welcome your comments and suggestions about Time Inc. Books.
Please write to us at:

Time Inc. Books
Attention: Book Editors
P.O. Box 62310, Tampa, FL 33662-2310
(800) 765-6400

*timeincbooks.com*

Time Inc. Books products may be purchased for business or
promotional use. For information on bulk purchases, please
contact Christi Crowley in the Special Sales Department at
(845) 895-9858.

There is a glossary at the end of this book.
This is an alphabetical list of words
and their definitions. The first time
a word that is in the glossary is
used, it appears in **bold**.

# CONTENTS

# BODY OF THE BEAST

Different dolphins have different body shapes and colorings, but all dolphins have features in common. This is where these features are found on a bottlenose dolphin.

Dorsal fin

Peduncle

Flukes

Median notch

Blowhole

Eye

Melon

Ear

Teeth

Rostrum

Pectoral fins

A dolphin is born with a tiny bit of hair on its **rostrum** (RAHS-trum), its mouth area. The hair falls out soon after birth. A dolphin also has hair around its **blowhole**.

**TOGETHERNESS** Dolphins are very playful and social. They develop friendships that can last a lifetime. They often travel in pairs or in large groups called **pods**.

# WHAT MAKES A DOLPHIN A DOLPHIN?

Dolphins spend their whole lives in the water, but they are not fish. They're **warm-blooded** mammals, just like you. Dolphins belong to a group of animals called **cetaceans** (sih-TAY-shunz), which also includes whales and porpoises. Cetaceans are mammals that live *only* in the water.

There are 44 **species**, or types, of dolphin. Most live in the ocean, but 5 species of dolphin live in rivers.

(Scientists are still looking into the number of river dolphin species—there may be more, or some may be subspecies.) A dolphin has a thick layer of fat under its skin called **blubber**. Blubber helps keep the dolphin warm and helps it float. Blubber also stores energy, in the form of proteins and fats. This helps the dolphin go long stretches between meals.

Fish use body parts called **gills** to get oxygen from water. But a dolphin, like all mammals, uses lungs. It must swim to the surface of the water to breathe. The blowhole on the top of a dolphin's head is connected to its lungs.

Dolphins breathe two to three times

**BY A NOSE** A dolphin's rostrum might look like a big nose, but it has no nostrils. A dolphin uses it to poke along the sandy ocean floor as it is looking for food. The blowhole is the dolphin's nostril, but it has no sense of smell.

per minute. When they dive deep for food, they can hold their breath for more than ten minutes. However, dolphins don't breathe automatically. They have to think about breathing.

Dolphins look like floating logs when they sleep, so their deep sleep is called logging.

Dolphins can stay fully alert for 15 days straight. They nap while swimming in packs. When a dolphin needs a deeper sleep, it floats with its blowhole above the water's surface. Half the dolphin's brain is awake at all times to keep the animal from drowning in its sleep.

Female dolphins give birth to live young. A female dolphin has one baby, called a **calf**, at a time. It grows inside its mother's body for 12 months. An Atlantic bottlenose dolphin calf is about 40 to 50 inches long at birth and weighs between 20 and 40 pounds. Like all mammals, baby dolphins drink their mothers' milk. To nurse, a calf rolls its tongue into a cone shape and latches onto its mother's teat

**FIRST BREATH** Shortly after giving birth, the mother guides her baby to the surface to breathe.

(nipple). The milk has a high fat content. This helps the calf build up its blubber so it can swim more easily.

Dolphins are **carnivores**. This means they eat meat. Whether they live and hunt near the coast in shallow waters, out at sea, or in a river, dolphins often work in teams to round up their meals.

Dolphins have special organs, called **melons**, on their foreheads. The melons allow the dolphins to **echolocate**, sending clicking sounds out into the water. Dolphins can find objects, including prey, in the water around them by listening for echoes

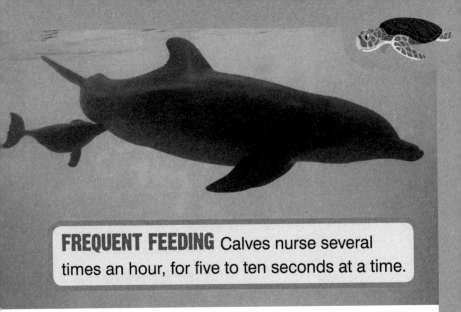

**FREQUENT FEEDING** Calves nurse several times an hour, for five to ten seconds at a time.

as the clicks bounce back.

Dolphins communicate with each other through whistles, clicks, and body language. Their brains are very large, compared to the sizes of their bodies. Scientists think that animals with relatively large brains have greater intelligence. Dolphins are second only to humans in brain size compared to body size.

**Dolphins share similar features,** but they don't all look alike. The Maui's dolphin is the smallest, at 4 to 5.5 feet long. The largest in the dolphin family is the orca (killer whale). An orca can grow to 30 feet long!

## WHITE-BEAKED

This dolphin has a short, stocky beak. The beak may be white, gray, or

black, but the tip is always white. This dolphin can grow up to 10 feet long.

## LONG-BEAKED COMMON This

dolphin has a white belly with a yellowish strip that forms a bold pattern on its side. It can grow up to 8 feet long.

**DUSKY** With a bluish-black back and two-toned fins, this dolphin can grow up to 6.5 feet long.

**ATLANTIC SPOTTED** This dolphin develops spots as it ages. The spots are darker on the belly than on the back. The Atlantic spotted dolphin can grow up to 7.5 feet long.

**HOURGLASS** Named for the hourglass-shaped pattern on its body, this dolphin can grow up to 6 feet long.

**GROUP ACTIVITY** Spinner dolphins can travel in small numbers or in large groups of a thousand or more.

# POD LIFE

Dolphins live in groups called pods. Dolphins in pods work together to hunt for food, avoid or fight off **predators**, and find mates. Pods can consist of just a few dolphins, or thousands.

A dolphin doesn't stick to one pod for life. Members of the group often split up and go separate ways. They join different groups depending on age, whether they are male or female, and whether they are having babies. Pairs or smaller groups may team up to achieve particular goals as well.

**NURSERY PODS** Pregnant females, new mothers, and calves live in nursery pods. Adult females, called **cows**, give birth about every three years. Dolphins are born throughout the year. Sometimes another female dolphin, known as an "auntie," will help a mother give birth or look after her calf. The auntie might be the only other dolphin the new mother allows near her calf. Some cows are more protective than others. A calf nurses for up to two years, sometimes from female dolphins in the pod other than its mother.

A calf sticks close to its mother. It often swims just above and to the side of the cow, in her **slipstream**. The slipstream is the

flow of water behind the cow that moves at the same speed she is swimming. Swimming in its mother's slipstream helps the calf keep up. And it helps both mother and calf stay with the pod.

A mother calls out to her calf continually in the days after birth. Over the first six months of life, a calf develops its own signature whistle. No other dolphin uses the same whistle. The calf's signature whistle is very similar to the sound its mother uses to call to it. The mother, or another dolphin, calls out the signature whistle, and the calf repeats it back.

Dolphins use their signature whistles throughout their lives. These calls help dolphins locate each other in their pods. They also allow dolphins to introduce themselves in a friendly way to dolphins they don't know.

The bond between mother and calf lasts a lifetime, but calves wander farther away as they get older. They form relationships with other **juvenile** (JOO-vuh-nile), or young, dolphins. When they are old enough, young male and female dolphins form pods together. Through play, they learn social rules, teamwork, and who's who in the group. From time to time,

**PLAYTIME!** Calves like to explore and play with kelp (seaweed).

juveniles will leave their groups to visit with their mothers.

Female dolphins reach adulthood at different ages, depending on the species and where they live. They are considered adults when they are old enough to have babies. Pregnant females often return to their mothers' nursery pods.

**BOY BONDS** Adult males stay in tight-knit groups for many years. Often, two male dolphins will form a close bond called an

## HOW DO DOLPHINS MAKE NOISES?

A dolphin takes in air through its blowhole. The air returns from the lungs into air sacs that sit below the blowhole. The air is forced over **tissue**, which **vibrates** (moves back and forth very quickly) and creates a sound.

**alliance** (uh-LYE-ints). This relationship can last throughout their lives. When two or more alliances join forces, they create a **coalition** (koh-uh-LISH-un). Male coalitions form in order to fight off rival groups and guard potential mates.

A male dolphin will show his **dominance** through body language such as tail slapping, or by chasing a rival off or raking

another dolphin's skin with his teeth. But dolphins don't hold grudges. Two dolphins, or even two rival coalitions, may fight one day. The next day, they set aside their differences to work together. Humans and other **primates** (such as chimpanzees) often hold a "me first" mentality. Dolphins, in contrast, will work with others if that helps them meet their needs.

Young dolphins learn through play. This group is engaged in "mock combat" (play fighting).

## FIN-GER PRINTS

Researchers can identify dolphins by their unique **dorsal** (DOR-sul) fins. The size and shape of a dorsal fin, and the notches in it, act like a fingerprint. Like fingerprints, no two fins are exactly the same. Researchers keep photos of each dolphin. Experienced scientists can instantly recognize each dolphin in a pod that they are studying. Dolphins do get new nicks in their fins from time to time. The researchers update their photos when they spot a change in a dolphin's fin.

Risso's dolphin

Orca

Bottlenose dolphin

Spotted dolphin

Commerson's dolphin

**CHOMP!** A dolphin can have from as few as 32 teeth to as many as 250, depending on the species. Bottlenose dolphins, such as this one, have 80 to 100 teeth.

# HUNTING HABITS

Dolphins have cone-shaped teeth, but they don't chew their food. Their feeding style is often described as "grab, bite, and swallow." They capture their prey with their teeth and swallow those tasty fish whole. Dolphins enjoy different types of fish, depending on the season. And sometimes they eat **crustaceans** (kruh-STAY-shunz)—such as lobsters, shrimp, and crabs—or squid. Dolphins use different hunting **tactics** based on where they are and what they

Strand feeding

are hunting. Sometimes dolphins work in teams; at other times they hunt alone.

In the marshy waters of South Carolina and Georgia, bottlenose dolphins swim into very shallow water at low tide. They **herd** fish toward the shore. Then they rush at the fish, creating a wave of water. The fish flop onto land, and the dolphins **strand** themselves on the shore to feed.

**DINNERTIME!** Dolphins have other creative hunting techniques to use when it's time to eat.

**KERPLUNKING** Dolphins hunting in seagrass slap their flukes, making *kerplunk* sounds. The noise startles fish out of their hiding spots.

**FISH WHACKING** Dolphins use their tails to whip fish 30 feet into the air.

**CRATER FEEDING** Dolphins use their rostrums to dig out treats from under the sand.

If they get stuck on land, they could die. But they wiggle back into the water every

## HOW DOES ECHOLOCATION WORK?

Dolphins use echolocation to "see" objects from as far as 100 feet away. First, a dolphin makes clicking noises inside its head. The melon in its head focuses the sound into a narrow beam. The dolphin rapidly moves its head from side to side.

The clicks bounce off objects in the water, sending **sound waves** back to the dolphin. The dolphin feels the echoes in its lower jaw. The reflected sounds make pictures for the dolphin. It can tell the size, shape, distance, and speed of prey, and even the type of fish it is. The dolphin can even identify wood, metal, and plastic objects such as piers and boats.

time. Leftovers are quickly gobbled up by birds nearby.

In Australia, a small number of female bottlenose dolphins have mastered **hydroplaning** (HIGH-droh-play-ning). They swim at high speeds, chasing fish very close to the shoreline. The dolphins expertly glide on the surface of the water. The fish struggle in the shallows and become an easy meal.

Hydroplaning

Bottlenose dolphins use a team tactic called **mud ringing** to catch schools of mullet fish in the shallow waters of the Gulf of Mexico. One dolphin, called a net maker, swims in a circle to stir up mud on the seafloor. The fish are trapped within the mud and swim to the surface. Another dolphin calls in the rest of the hunting pod. The panicked fish leap out of the water, into the mouths of waiting dolphins.

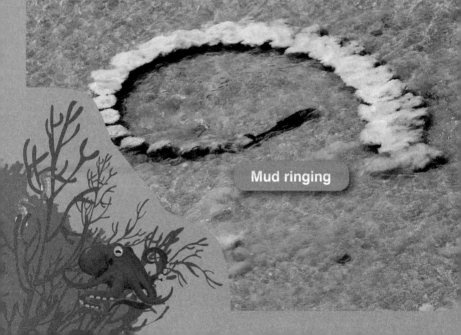

Mud ringing

Bait ball

Some small fish, such as sardines, herring, and anchovies, travel in large schools for protection. The way the schools move looks a bit like a flowing river, so scientists call these moving schools streams. Unfortunately for the fish, large schools attract hungry predators. When danger approaches, the small fish in a school swim together into a tight formation called a **bait ball**. If dolphins were to swim right in and start eating, the school would scatter. So the dolphins team up in a hunting method called bait

When closer to shore, dolphins may **corral** fish in shallow waters. When the fish jump out of the water to escape, the dolphins catch and eat them. Dolphins have teeth, but they don't chew their food. It's grab, bite, and down the hatch!

balling. One dolphin swims below the bait ball to prevent fish from escaping. Other dolphins swim in circles around the bait ball to keep the fish inside. Dolphins take turns swimming into the bait ball to eat. When feasts like this are over, the dolphins leap into the air, chatter, and touch one another. It looks like a celebration!

## IS THAT FOOD?

Many fish and amphibians can sense the electrical pulses given off by all living things. This sense is called **electroreception** (ih-lek-troh-rih-SEP-shun). Some dolphins have it, too. While echolocation helps dolphins find things that are farther away, electroreception helps locate nearby food, such as flounder buried in the sand.

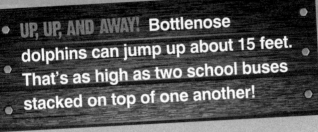

**UP, UP, AND AWAY!** Bottlenose dolphins can jump up about 15 feet. That's as high as two school buses stacked on top of one another!

# CHAPTER 4

# MOVING AROUND

Dolphins are designed for power, speed, and agility (the ability to move quickly and easily). They have front limbs called **pectoral** (PEK-tuh-rul) fins, or flippers. Although dolphins don't have fingers, the flippers have finger bones inside them. Dolphins use their flippers to steer themselves in different directions.

The tail of a dolphin has two **lobes**, or parts, called flukes. The flukes don't have bones—they are made of tough tissue. Muscles in the dolphin's back move the flukes to help with swimming. The dorsal fin is also made of tough tissue. This fin is usually located on a dolphin's back. It keeps the dolphin steady and prevents it from spinning constantly when it's moving at high speeds.

A powerful set of muscles runs from a dolphin's head to its tail. Between the muscle layer and the skin is the blubber layer. Blubber keeps the dolphin warm, but it is also springy. The springy blubber helps the dolphin's muscles work hard without using too much energy.

A dolphin has a tubelike shape that is pointed at both ends. Its skin is **sleek** (smooth) and hairless. These features help water

flow easily over its body.

Fish move their tails from side to side as they swim. But dolphins move their powerful **peduncles** (PEE-dung-kulz)—

tail areas—up and down. They arch and relax their backs to propel themselves through the water at average speeds of 3 to 7 miles per hour. With their

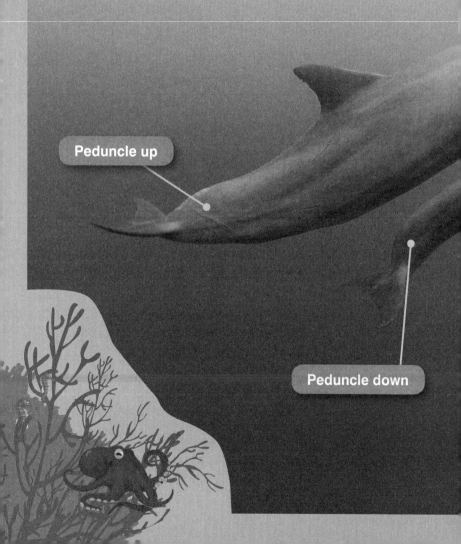

Peduncle up

Peduncle down

powerful muscles and sleek bodies, bottlenose dolphins can reach speeds of more than 20 miles per hour for short bursts.

**JUMPING HIGH** When preparing to jump out of the water, a dolphin first swims deep. Then it picks up speed as it races back to the surface. It can blast more than 15 feet into the air and even perform complete somersaults.

**TWIST AND SPIN** Spinner dolphins can make as many as seven **rotations**, or complete turns, during one leap. Spinning may help these dolphins get rid of **remora** (rih-MOR-uh) fish that are suctioned onto their bodies. Or the spinning could be a way to show happiness or get attention from other dolphins.

**RIDING THE WAVES** Sailors often see dolphins swimming in the **bow** waves in front of boats. Dolphins ride these waves just like a surfer would. The waves carry them, which may help the dolphins save energy while traveling.

## DOLPHIN SUPERPOWERS

They don't wear capes, but dolphins have special features that make them amazing creatures of the sea.

**EXCELLENT EYESIGHT** A dolphin's eyes are on the sides of its head, so it can see nearly all around. Each eye can move independently, which means a dolphin can look forward and backward at the same time.

**SUPER SKIN** Dolphins grow completely new skin every two hours. A gel that coats the skin prevents **barnacles** (BAR-nuh-kuhls) and **bacteria** (bak-TEER-ee-uh) from attaching to their bodies. This helps them glide smoothly through the water.

**DEEP BREATHING** When you breathe, you replace about 15 percent of the air in your lungs. Dolphins replace nearly 80 percent of the air in their lungs with each breath. This means they can get oxygen faster. It is one of the reasons they can dive deep and hold their breath while underwater.

**WHO'S THAT?** Scientists who study animal intelligence often test animals to see whether they can pass the mirror test (recognize themselves). In addition to bottlenose dolphins, only humans, great apes, elephants, and magpies have passed.

# BRAINPOWER

Dolphins are smart! They seem to be able to figure things out quickly and pass on what they learn to other dolphins. As babies, they start out by **imitating**, or copying, their mothers. They learn how to swim, how to breathe, and how to call to each other. They continue to learn through imitation their whole lives.

Dolphins can even imitate people. When a bottlenose dolphin in an aquarium saw divers cleaning the glass in its tank, it found a feather and started wiping the glass in the same way.

Using tools is considered a sign of intelligence in animals. Elephants use branches to swat at flies, and gorillas use sticks when they need to see how deep water is. In Shark Bay, off the coast of Australia, Indo-Pacific bottlenose dolphins have been spotted swimming with sea sponges on their snouts. Dolphins that use sponges in this way are known as spongers. Research has shown that spongers eat different foods than non-spongers do. Spongers tend to eat food from the ocean floor, where bottom-dwelling fish may be harder to find using echolocation. When dolphins poke along the ocean

floor looking for tasty treats, sharp rocks and spiny sea creatures such as urchins and stingrays could hurt their noses. So these dolphins figured out a clever way to protect themselves.

Dolphins show their smarts in other ways, too. They have good problem-solving skills. This is clear from the different ways they hunt and organize pods with strong leaders. They also seem to remember one another over long periods of time. But how intelligent are they, really? Research

**RECESS!** Dolphins' playfulness is also a sign of their intelligence.

**JUST LIKE TOYS** Spinner dolphins off the coast of Hawaii play with leaves. They put them on their flippers, flukes, and dorsal fins. They pass them to one another, too. And some dolphins play with seaweed. They catch it, put it on their flukes, and swim around with it.

**BLOWING BUBBLES** Bubbles form naturally when dolphins let air through their blowholes. But sometimes a dolphin seems to be playing with the bubbles. It pushes out a lot of bubbles quickly. The bubbles form one big, round bubble that opens into a ring as it rises to the surface. Then the dolphin plays with the big bubble ring.

gives us some answers.

Denise Herzing is a marine mammalogist (a scientist who studies mammals that live in the sea). She has been studying the behavior of Atlantic spotted dolphins in the wild. She and her team of scientists have compiled a long list of dolphin sound patterns. They created an underwater computer called a CHAT box. CHAT creates and records sounds in an effort to understand and "talk" to dolphins. The Wild Dolphin Project has been going on for 30 years, and Dr. Herzing hopes one day to crack the code of dolphin language.

Another study tested whether dolphins could work together to figure out how to solve a problem. Researchers

**LEARN AND EARN**

## CLEVER DOLPHIN!

At the Institute for Marine Mammal Studies in Mississippi, dolphins are trained to clean up the litter (trash) in their pools. When a dolphin gives a piece of litter to the trainer, it gets a fish. A dolphin named Kelly figured out that a small piece of litter got the same reward as a larger piece. So she stored large pieces of paper and tore off smaller pieces for more rewards.

put fish in a closed container with ropes at either end. They assumed two dolphins would need to team up—one pulling each rope—to open the container and get the food. Two dolphins figured out how to open the container in just 30 seconds. Amazingly, one dolphin figured

out how to do it on its own!

The scientists heard the
dolphins chattering to one another
during the study. They wondered if the
animals were "talking" about how to
solve the puzzle. No one knows for sure.

We still have a lot to learn about
how their brains work. But it's clear
that dolphins are some of the smartest
animals on Earth.

**BY THE SHORE** Most dolphins live in shallow waters where the water is warm and food is plentiful.

# OCEAN BUDDIES

Dolphins can be found in almost all the oceans on Earth. In oceans, they mostly live in shallow waters, along the coasts of different **continents**. This coastal area is called the **continental shelf**. Some bottlenose dolphins also live offshore, or out in the open ocean, far from land.

Coastal and offshore dolphins have different body types. Coastal bottlenose dolphins are lighter in color and smaller than dolphins that live in the open ocean, and they have larger flippers. The larger flippers allow coastal dolphins to get around in shallow waters. Shallow waters are warmer, so coastal dolphins also have less blubber than offshore dolphins in colder waters do. Some dolphins that live in colder waters **migrate** (MYE-grate), or move, to warmer waters when the seasons change.

Bryde's whale

## ATLANTIC OCEAN HABITAT

Bottlenose dolphins share their Atlantic Ocean habitat (home) with Bryde's (BROO-duhz) whales, seals, and jellyfish such as sea nettles. In this habitat, the dolphins' favorite meals include fish such as herring, halibut, mullet, and cod. They also eat squid, and bottom-feeders such as lobsters and crabs. Their only predators are orcas, great white sharks, and tiger sharks.

Sea nettle

Harbor seal

**PACIFIC OCEAN HABITAT** Otters, seals, and sea lions can be found in the bottlenose dolphin's Pacific Ocean habitat. Many whale species, including the giant blue whale, also make their home here. Large fish such as tuna and swordfish roam the open ocean, along

Blue whale

Bluefin tuna

with barracuda and several salmon species. Dolphins mostly feast on the herring and mackerel also found here.

Sea lion

Swordfish

Sea otter

**CARIBBEAN HABITAT** Short-beaked common dolphins share busy coral reefs with sea turtles, as well as sea urchins and sea stars. In deeper tropical waters, dolphins share the sea with giant whale sharks. Other tropical animals include blue marlins, moray eels, hammerhead sharks, and manta rays.

**INDO-PACIFIC HABITAT** Indo-Pacific bottlenose dolphins generally stick to shallow coastal waters on the continental shelf or around islands in the Indian and central Pacific Oceans. They feed on a wide variety of fish, squid, and octopuses.

**ANTARCTIC HABITAT** Hourglass dolphins have **adapted** (changed) to survive in the frigid Antarctic waters. They enjoy small fish, crustaceans, and squid. They feed at the surface of the water. Adélie (uh-DEL-ee) and emperor penguins live on the icy edge of the continent.

Adélie penguins

**IN LIVING COLOR** Amazon River dolphins are born with gray skin. As they get older, their skin gets paler and they look pink, or pink and gray.

# RIVER ROVERS

Some dolphins live in rivers, on the continents of South America and Asia. River dolphins have bodies that are adapted for their river habitats. Some live only in freshwater (water that is not salty), found in rivers and lakes. Others can live in both freshwater and the salty water found where rivers meet oceans.

Unlike ocean dolphins, river dolphins have free-floating **vertebrae** (VUR-tuh-bray) in their necks. (Vertebrae are bones in an animal's back that form the spinal column.) This gives river dolphins great **flexibility** and allows them to make sharp turns in shallow waters.

River dolphins need less blubber to live in warmer river waters. They are slower swimmers than oceanic dolphins are. Also, their vision doesn't help them get around in **murky** (dark and cloudy) river waters. Instead, they rely on echolocation to navigate, or find their way.

River dolphins are rapidly losing their habitats. Boat traffic, fishing, human population growth, and pollution all pose threats.

Let's take a closer look at different river dolphin species.

## AMAZON RIVER DOLPHIN Also

known as the boto (BOH-too) or pink
river dolphin, this is the largest freshwater
dolphin. Amazon River dolphins have
pale pink skin and extremely long snouts.
They can grow to 350 pounds and 8 feet
long. They live in the Amazon and Orinoco
Rivers in South America.

Amazon River dolphin

Experts aren't sure exactly why Amazon River dolphins become pink as they get older. It may be because the blood in their bodies shows through as the skin becomes paler. Amazon River dolphins turn a brighter pink when they get excited, the way humans do when they blush.

**GANGES RIVER DOLPHIN** Ganges (GAN-jeez) River dolphins live in river systems in India, Nepal, and Bangladesh. They have **stocky** (short and thick) bodies and light gray-brown skin. Their flippers are large, but their dorsal fins are very small. They have limited vision—they can detect only the direction of light.

Ganges River dolphin

Ganges River dolphins are **solitary** animals. This means they travel alone. There are fewer than 1,800 Ganges River dolphins alive today.

**INDUS RIVER DOLPHIN** Scientists disagree about whether Indus River dolphins are the same species as Ganges River dolphins or their own separate species. These dolphins live in the Indus River in Pakistan. Like the Ganges River

Indus River dolphin

dolphin, the Indus River dolphin is blind and can detect only light. Scientists estimate that just 1,100 Indus River dolphins exist today.

**BAIJI** The baiji (BYE-jee) is shy and graceful. It travels in small groups, in the Yangtze (YANG-see) River in China. Little else is known about this species. The last time one was spotted was in

Baiji

2002, and it may now be extinct.

**IRRAWADDY DOLPHIN** The dark gray
Irrawaddy (ir-uh-WAH-dee) dolphin has
a rounded head and no beak. It has a
tiny dorsal fin and **broad** (wide) flippers.
Irrawaddy dolphins usually travel in
groups of fewer than 6, but sometimes up
to 15 dolphins will travel together. They
can be found in river systems in Southeast
Asia, from the Philippines to India.

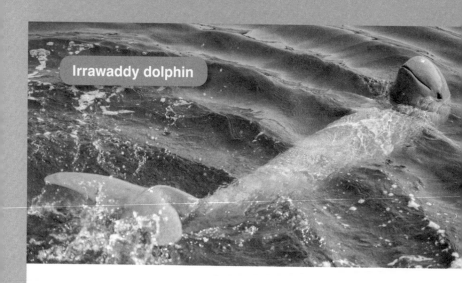
Irrawaddy dolphin

**TUCUXI** Small and dark gray, tucuxis (too-COO-zeez) are not true river dolphins. They are members of the same family as oceanic dolphins. However, they can live in both fresh and salty water and are often seen in the Amazon and

Tucuxi

Orinoco Rivers. Tucuxis travel in close groups of about 15 dolphins.

**LA PLATA DOLPHIN** The coastal La Plata (lah PLAH-tah) dolphin is found in **estuaries** (ES-choo-er-eez), where fresh and salty waters mix. It has a small, slender (thin) body and resembles the tucuxi. The La Plata dolphin is the dolphin with the longest beak relative to body size—its beak is nearly one-sixth of its body length.

Rescued La Plata dolphin calf

# FIN FACT

## EXTREME DOLPHINS

### FASTEST
**Dall's porpoise** Up to 34.5 miles per hour, tied with orca.

### SLOWEST
**Amazon River dolphin**
1 to 2 miles per hour

### MOST ACROBATIC
**Dusky dolphin**

## BEST JUMPER
**Spinner dolphin**
15 feet in the air, while spinning up to 7 times

## LONGEST
**Orca**
Up to 30 feet

## SHORTEST
**Maui's dolphin**
About 4 feet

**I SPY** Orcas poke their heads above water to find out what's going on above the surface. They move their tail flukes back and forth to hold their bodies upright, the way people kick their legs to tread water.

# ORCAS AND OTHERS

t may surprise you to learn that the dolphin family includes several species that are called whales. Orcas (also called killer whales), false killer whales, pilot whales, and melon-headed whales are all what are known as toothed whales, which belong to the dolphin family.

Toothed whales differ from the larger, krill-eating baleen (bay-LEEN) whales in a number of ways. The differences include body size, how they hunt, and what they eat.

Here are ways experts decide whether a whale is a toothed whale or a baleen whale.

## TOOTHED WHALES

**BLOWHOLE:** A toothed whale has one blowhole, just like its dolphin relatives.

**TONGUE:** Toothed whales have small tongues.

**HUNTING:** A toothed whale uses echolocation to hunt prey. It grabs prey with its teeth, then swallows it whole. Toothed whales eat larger fish and even other marine mammals.

**SIZE:** Toothed whales can be small to large, and the males are usually larger than the females.

## BALEEN WHALES

**BLOWHOLE:** A baleen whale has two blowholes.

**TONGUE:** Baleen whales have large tongues.

**HUNTING:** A baleen whale eats plankton (tiny ocean animals) and small fish. It opens its mouth and lets water pour through its baleen plates. These are made of the same material

Tongue

your fingernails are. The baleen filters small animals out of the water, sending the food down the whale's throat and the water back into the ocean.

**SIZE:** Baleen whales tend to be large, and the females are usually larger than the males.

**ORCAS** These are the largest members of the oceanic dolphin family. They are considered dolphins because they have cone-shaped teeth and curved dorsal fins. Like dolphins, orcas have melons, which help them with echolocation.

These dolphins are found all over the world. They live in pods and work together to hunt for food. Mothers and calves form strong bonds that last a lifetime.

Orcas swim up to 30 miles per hour. They prey on almost any animal that lives in or at the edge of the sea. Orcas have 40 to 56 teeth that are up to 4 inches long. These help them hunt large animals.

**FALSE KILLER WHALES** These whales look similar to orcas, and they, too, are members of the oceanic dolphin family. Playful and social, these dolphins travel in pods of 10 to 50 individuals.

**PILOT WHALES** There are two species of pilot whale: long-finned pilot whales and short-finned pilot whales. Each has only 40 to 48 teeth, far fewer than the 120 teeth most dolphins have. Long-finned

Long-finned pilot whales

pilot whales have very long flippers.
Both species travel in close-knit pods
of 10 to 20 members. Pods sometimes
join together in schools of hundreds of
dolphins. Short-finned pilot whales
like warm tropical and **temperate**
waters, and long-finned pilot
whales stay in cooler waters.
Both species may be
seen floating at the

surface, spy-hopping, or surfing the waves behind boats.

**MELON-HEADED WHALES** A melon-headed whale has a distinct head shape. It doesn't have a beak, and its head is gently curved. Its tube-shaped body is narrow at the tail. Melon-headed whales usually travel in groups of 100 to 500 members. But pods have been seen with up to 2,000 individuals.

Melon-headed whales

# FACT FILE: ON PORPOISE

**Porpoises are relatives of dolphins** and toothed whales. They do not belong to the dolphin family, but they are cetaceans. Here's a look at a few.

Harbor porpoises are found mostly in northern Europe. They have small flippers and no beaks.

Finless porpoises have round heads and no dorsal fins. They live in the coastal waters of Southeast Asia.

Dall's porpoises prefer the cold waters of the northern Pacific. They have sloping foreheads. Their dorsal fins have hooked tips.

Vaquitas (vuh-KEE-tuhz) are the most endangered marine animals. Their name means "little cow," due to their chubby bodies. The small population of vaquitas lives in the shallow waters off the coast of Mexico, in the Gulf of California.

**LEARNING AND DOING** A dolphin first experiences helping when its mother guides it to the surface to start breathing. Adult dolphins not only help their own **offspring**, they sometimes help people and other animals.

# DOLPHIN DO-GOODERS

Dolphins often use their communication skills, strength, teamwork, and excellent hearing to perform kind deeds. Some scientists are not sure if dolphins are actually showing care and concern at these times. They think that dolphins benefit in some way from their acts of kindness.

In Mahia Beach, New Zealand, two local men were struggling to save a stranded pygmy sperm whale and her calf. The animals were stuck in shallow water between a sandbar and the shore. The men had been trying to help for more than an hour, but the whales couldn't find their way around the sandbar. Suddenly Moko, a playful bottlenose dolphin often seen in the area, showed up. She swam between the two men and the whales. She guided the whales to a deep part of the water, where they were able to swim back out to sea.

From 1888 to 1912, a Risso's dolphin met ships in Pelorus (puh-LOR-us) Sound, New Zealand. The dolphin was given the name Pelorus Jack, after this body of water. He loved to ride the ships' bow waves. It was said that Pelorus Jack guided ships through the rough and rocky area of

**HELPERS IN THE OCEAN**

## WHO GUARDS THE LIFEGUARDS?

Sometimes dolphins know people need help even before they do. In 2004, four lifeguards were swimming off the coast of New Zealand when the dolphins around them suddenly began acting very strangely. The dolphins formed tight circles around the group and slapped the water with their tails. They were herding the lifeguards close together. Were the dolphins being friendly or angry? Then the lifeguards realized that a shark nearly 10 feet long was circling nearby. For 40 minutes, the dolphins protected the group. Finally a patrol boat noticed the dolphins' behavior and rescued the lifeguards.

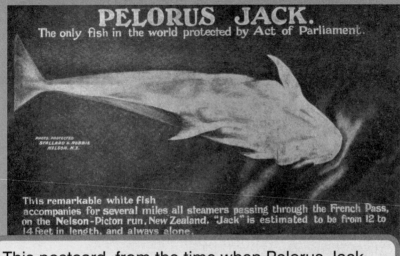

This postcard, from the time when Pelorus Jack patrolled the waters of Pelorus Sound, is an indication of his fame in New Zealand and beyond.

water called French Pass. World-famous writers Mark Twain and Rudyard Kipling traveled all the way to New Zealand just to see Pelorus Jack in action.

Some say Pelorus Jack was a hero. Others think he was just lonely or bored, as Risso's dolphins were rarely seen in the area and

he did not have a pod for company.

Surfer Todd Endris credited dolphins with saving his life. He was surfing off Monterey, California, in 2007 when a great white shark bit him. While he was trying to fight off the shark, Todd noticed dolphins swimming around him. They quickly created a wall between him and the shark. The dolphins' actions stopped the shark attack and allowed Todd to make it back to shore. Todd's friends pulled him out, and he survived.

Todd Endris shows the scars from his shark encounter.

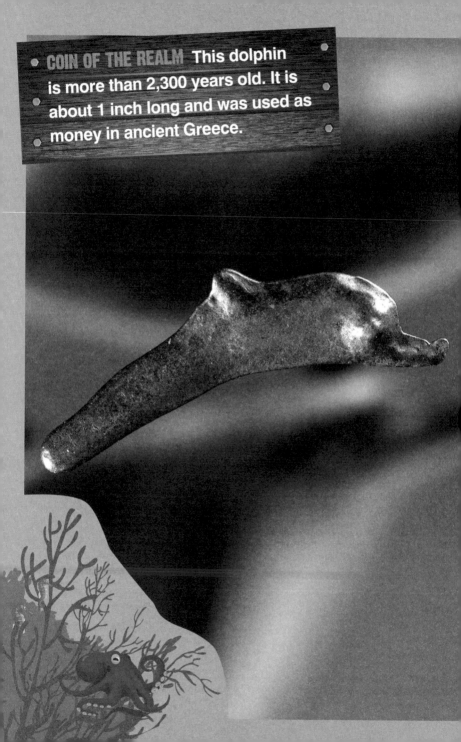

**COIN OF THE REALM** This dolphin is more than 2,300 years old. It is about 1 inch long and was used as money in ancient Greece.

# ANCIENT MARINERS

**A**ncient Greece was a **seafaring** culture. The people used the sea to travel from place to place. **Mariners** (MER-uh-nurz), or sailors, often faced dangers at sea. They were very superstitious and believed in gods and magic to explain the unknown. To sailors, dolphins riding the bow waves of boats seemed to be messengers from the gods. And stories of dolphins rescuing sailors lost at sea are plentiful in Greek literature.

These sea creatures were a very important part of ancient Greek culture and appear in many myths from that time.

**ARION AND THE DOLPHINS** One Greek myth (traditional story) tells the tale of Arion, a beloved musician. Everyone who heard Arion's voice stopped to listen. The king enjoyed his music so much that he ordered a ship to carry Arion to a music festival in Sicily, off the coast of what is now Italy. First prize would be a pot of gold.

Arion traveled to Sicily and, of course, won the festival. As he sailed back home, the ship's crew members became jealous of him. They decided that Arion must be killed so that they could keep his gold. Arion pleaded for his life, but the captain would not change his mind. So

Arion asked only that he be allowed to sing one last song before he died. The captain agreed. Arion sang so sweetly that dolphins gathered near the boat. As he sang his last note, he leaped overboard.

The crew sailed on, thinking Arion would die in the water. Instead, the dolphins carried him to land. When the king learned what had happened, he

**banished** (sent away as punishment) the captain and crew. Arion carried on singing in the kingdom, and whenever he did, dolphins gathered near the shore.

## APOLLO AND THE TEMPLE AT DELPHI

In another myth, the god Apollo disguised himself as a dolphin and jumped onto a merchant ship. He took the crew members **hostage** and forced them all to become his servants. Apollo traveled to the island of Pytho, where he planned to build his temple. He changed the name of the island to Delphi (DEL-fye), which means "dolphin." The ruins of the ancient Temple of Apollo at Delphi still stand today.

Temple of Apollo

## TARAS, THE BOY RIDING A DOLPHIN

In this story, Taras, the son of the god of the sea, was rescued from a shipwreck by a dolphin that his father sent. The dolphin brought Taras ashore to a city in what is now the south of Italy. The city was named Taras in his honor; today it is called Taranto. An ancient silver coin shows Taras riding on the back of a dolphin.

# FACT FILE: TIME TRAVEL

**Evidence of people's fascination** and relationship with dolphins can be found in practical and decorative objects from ancient civilizations.

**LEPTIS MAGNA**
These ruins from Leptis Magna, an ancient city in Libya, North Africa, were once the legs of stalls at the marketplace.

**SABRATHA** About 1,800 years ago, these ancient dolphins **adorned** the stage of a theater in the port city of Sabratha, in Libya.

**KNOSSOS** This dolphin **fresco** (a painting on plaster) can be seen in the ancient ruins of the Palace of Minos at Knossos, on the Greek island of Crete.

**MEXICO** Some 3,000 years ago, the ancient Olmec civilization thrived along the Gulf of Mexico. Many Olmec stone statues, including this dolphin, survive today.

**DEADLY CATCH** Humans catch and remove more than 100 million tons of fish from the world's oceans every year. If there aren't enough fish, dolphins struggle to find enough food to eat.

# SAVING DOLPHINS

**D**olphins have few predators in the wild. Unfortunately, humans pose the greatest danger to them. From eating habits to energy use, human behavior threatens the survival of dolphins and many other marine species.

**FISHING** **Commercial** (business) fishing boats often use gill nets—large, wall-like panels of netting that catch lots of fish at once. Gill nets are hard for dolphins to see or locate through echolocation. This

Gill net

means dolphins can get tangled in the nets and drown. Animals that get caught in nets that are meant for different types of animals are called **bycatch**. To reduce bycatch, there are rules for gill net fishing in some places. For example, in California and along the East Coast from Maine to New Jersey, fishing boats are required to have

**acoustic** (sound) devices to warn cetaceans.

**CLIMATE CHANGE** Human activities contribute to global warming, or climate change. These activities include burning **fossil fuels** (oil and gas) and **deforestation** (cutting down forests). A lot of the warmth added by climate change is absorbed by ocean waters. Rising sea temperatures mean that the fish and plants that live in the ocean have to adapt.

Living reef

Dying reef

As ocean temperatures rise, coral reefs die off. Fish that live around them must move to cooler waters. Dolphins that feed on the reef fish move away, too, as food becomes scarce (hard to find). If they can't adapt fast enough, whole marine populations may be reduced in number or die off.

**NOISE POLLUTION** Shipping and marine industries and military activities introduce powerful, loud noises into the oceans. Dolphins use their hearing to figure out where they are and where to go, so loud sounds can cause them to become disoriented (confused). Often, groups of whales lose their way and get stuck near shore or on

beaches. Scientists think that some mass strandings are due to the loud noises.

**WATER POLLUTION** Plastic bags and packaging, discarded nets, and other pieces of garbage left in the ocean can harm dolphins when they swallow or become tangled in them. Trash on the street can wash into storm drains when

it rains and end up in rivers or streams
that lead to oceans. This means
that a paper cup or candy
wrapper dropped hundreds of
miles away can become
ocean pollution. And

industrial waste causes ocean pollution, too. This can include oils and different chemicals, such as pesticides for bugs and fertilizers for plants. They spill into oceans and rivers, accidentally or on purpose, and can harm marine life and habitats.

## IN YOUR NEWSFEED

### KIDS KEEP TRACK

**WATCH AND RECORD**

Dolphins and whales often swim near islands off the coast of Scotland. According to a BBC (British Broadcasting Corporation) report, kids there have teamed up with the Whale and Dolphin Conservation Shorewatch. They will work together to record where they spot the animals. This will help experts locate and protect key areas such as the dolphins' **feeding grounds**.

# FACT FILE: FIVE WAYS YOU CAN HELP SAVE DOLPHINS

**There are things you can** do every day to make positive changes to reduce pollution, help stop climate change, and save dolphins.

**REDUCE** Turn off lights and appliances when you're not using them.

**REUSE** Always bring your own bags when shopping instead of using plastic bags.

**RECYCLE** Plastic, glass, aluminum, cardboard, and paper are all recyclable.

**CLEAN UP** Work with friends, school or community groups, and your family to organize a beach or community cleanup. This will keep trash from being carried by waterways out to the ocean. Or volunteer for the International Coastal Cleanup. Learn more at *oceanconservancy.org*.

**LEARN MORE** Read and learn more about human activities that affect the planet. Talk to your teacher about starting a class or community project to raise awareness about dolphins and the health of the oceans.

# GLOSSARY

**acoustic** Having to do with sound.

**adapt** To change behavior to make it easier to live in a particular place or situation.

**adorn** To decorate.

**alliance** A close bond between two male dolphins.

**bacteria** Tiny, single-celled organisms. Some bacteria can cause disease.

**bait ball** A group of small fish swimming closely together as protection against predators.

**banish** To force someone to leave a place and never return, as a punishment.

**barnacle** A small crustacean that permanently attaches itself to underwater surfaces, such as rocks and boats.

**blowhole** A hole for breathing at the top of a cetacean's head.

**blubber** The layer of fat under the skin of a large marine mammal. Dolphins, whales, and seals have blubber.

**bow** The front of a ship or boat.

**broad** Wide from side to side.

**bycatch** A fish or other marine animal that is caught unintentionally by commercial fishers.

**calf** A baby dolphin. Young animals of some other species—including cows, seals, and elephants—are also called calves.

**carnivore** An animal that eats meat.

**cetacean** Any member of a group of mammals that live only in the water. Dolphins, whales, and porpoises are cetaceans.

**coalition** A group formed when a pair of dolphins in an alliance joins forces with one or more other pairs.

**commercial** Having to do with business and making money.

**continent** One of seven large landmasses on Earth: Asia, Africa, Europe, North America, South America, Australia, and Antarctica.

**continental shelf** A shallow, sloping area of the ocean floor near the edge of a landmass.

**corral** To collect animals or things into an enclosed area.

**cow** An adult female dolphin. Adult females of some other species—including whales and elk—are also called cows.

**crustacean** A sea creature with an outer skeleton. Shrimp, crabs, and barnacles are crustaceans.

**deforestation** The clearing of forests, often over large areas.

**dominance** Power or influence over others.

**dorsal** Relating to, or located near or on, the back of animal. A dolphin's dorsal fin is on its back.

**echolocate** To use sound waves to find prey and other objects.

**electroreception** The ability to detect the electrical pulses given off by living things.

**estuary** An area where a river meets the ocean, and fresh and salty waters mix.

**feeding ground** A place where a group of animals regularly goes to find food.

**flexibility** The ability to bend easily.

**fossil fuel** A source of heat or energy (such as coal, oil, or natural gas) that is formed in the Earth from the remains of ancient plants or animals.

**fresco** A painting made on fresh, damp plaster on a wall or ceiling.

**gill** The part of a fish's body, near its mouth, through which it breathes by taking the oxygen from water.

**herd** To move animals from one place to another in a group.

**hostage** Someone or something held by a person who demands something, such as money, in exchange.

**hydroplaning** The act of gliding on the surface of water.

**imitate** To copy someone or something.

**juvenile** Young.

**lobe** A curved or rounded body part. A dolphin's tail has two lobes, called flukes.

**mariner** A sailor, especially one who steers or helps steer a ship.

**melon** A rounded organ in the front of a dolphin's head that is used in echolocation. Some other cetaceans also have melons.

**migrate** To move from one place to another according to the season.

**mud ringing** A cooperative feeding behavior used by bottlenose dolphins. They work together to stir up mud on the seafloor and trap fish inside the mud ring.

**murky** Cloudy, dark, or dirty.

**offspring** The young of an animal or person.

**pectoral** Relating to, or located near or on, the chest of an animal. A dolphin's pectoral fins are on the sides of its body.

**peduncle** The tail area of a dolphin.

**pod** A group of dolphins or whales that lives and travels together.

**predator** An animal that hunts and eats other animals.

**primate** Any member of the group of mammals that includes humans, apes, and monkeys.

**remora** A type of fish that has a suction disk on the top of its head, which it uses to attach itself to other fish.

**rostrum** The beaklike body part at the front of a dolphin's head.

**rotation** One complete turn.

**seafaring** Traveling by sea, or working on a boat.

**sleek** Smooth and glossy.

**slipstream** A flow of water directly behind a fast-moving object, such as a dolphin. The water moves at about the same speed as the object.

**solitary** Living alone, not needing the company of others.

**sound wave** A wave of energy, produced when something vibrates, that can be heard.

**species** A category of living things with similar traits that can mate and have offspring together. There are 44 different species of dolphin.

**spy-hop** To be upright in the water with the head sticking out to look around.

**stocky** Short, thick, and sturdy.

**strand** To force out of the water and leave stuck on shore.

**tactic** An action done to accomplish something specific.

**temperate** Having a moderate temperature, rarely either very high or very low.

**tissue** A group of similar cells that make up a particular part or organ of an animal or plant.

**vertebra** One of the small bones that make up the spine.

**vibrate** To move back and forth very quickly.

**warm-blooded** Able to maintain a constant body temperature regardless of the temperature of the environment. Dolphins, like all mammals, are warm-blooded.

# RESOURCES

Learn more about dolphins by reading more books, checking out interesting websites, and visiting various places where dolphins may be spotted in the wild.

## WHERE TO SEE WILD DOLPHINS

Dolphins are best seen from the shore or on a boat. Look for whale and dolphin-watch tours near you or when traveling to coastal communities. Here are just a few places and species to look for:

- In the United States, bottlenose dolphins frolic in temperate coastal waters—from Cape Cod to the Gulf of Mexico, off California, and around Hawaii.
- Large pods of spinner dolphins swim the waters around Hawaii.
- Atlantic white-sided dolphins swim off the Massachusetts coastline and near Nantucket Island
- Orcas and other whales swim off the coast of Alaska, including acrobatic humpbacks in Glacier Bay.

## WEBSITES

*mote.org/hospital/dolphin*
Learn about the Mote Marine Lab and their Dolphin & Whale, & Sea Turtle Hospital, and see how they treat live-stranded dolphins and whales and release them back into the wild.

*montereybayaquarium.org/animals-and-experiences/live-web-cams/monterey-bay-cam*
Live webcams of Monterey Bay and the open water give you a look at coastal marine life, including Pacific white-sided dolphins.

*oceanservice.noaa.gov/kids*
Start here to learn about marine life and habitats at informative and fun websites from the National Oceanic and Atmospheric Association.

*seewinter.com*
This website offers live webcams and a web series that takes you behind the scenes as the staff rescues, rehabilitates, and releases dolphins back into the wild. You can also visit this marine life rescue center at the Clearwater Marine Aquarium in Clearwater, Florida.

## BOOKS

*Animals: A Visual Encyclopedia*, by Animal Planet (Animal Planet/Time Inc. Books)

*Animal Bites: Ocean Animals*, by Animal Planet (Animal Planet/Time Inc. Books)

*Animal Planet Adventures: Dolphin Rescue*, by Catherine Nichols (Animal Planet/Time Inc. Books)

# INDEX

Illustrations are indicated by **boldface.** When they fall within a page span, the entire span is **boldface.**

# CREDITS AND ACKNOWLEDGMENTS

**Writer** Cari Jackson
**Produced by** Scout Books & Media Inc
**President and Project Director** Susan Knopf
**Project Manager** Brittany Gialanella
**Copyeditor** Stephanie Engel
**Proofreader** Melanie Petsch
**Designer** Annemarie Redmond
**Advisor** Andy Dehart, *VP of Animal Husbandry, Phillip and Patricia Frost Museum of Science*

**Thanks** to the Time Inc. Books team: Margot Schupf, Anja Schmidt, Beth Sutinis, Deirdre Langeland, Hillary Leary, Georgia Morrissey, Megan Pearlman, and Nina Reed.

**Special thanks** to everyone at Discovery Global Enterprises.

## PHOTO CREDITS

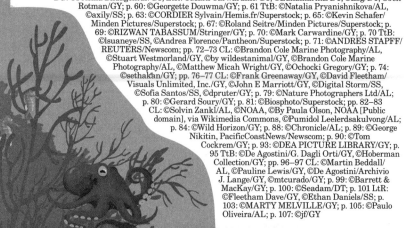